Copyright©

All rights reserved. This book may not be reproduced in any form, stored in a retrieval system, or transmitted in any form by any means—electronic, mechanical, photocopy, recording, or otherwise—without prior written permission of the publisher except in the case of brief quotations embodied in critical articles or reviews.

TABLE OF CONTENTS

INTRODUCTION **4**

GASLIGHTING **6**

What Is Gaslighting? 6

Why is Gaslighting so Terrible? 7

Tactics Used in Gaslighting 8

Signs You Are a Victim of Gaslighting 14

RECOGNIZING AND RESPONDING TO GASLIGHTING **19**

What to Do About It 19

How to Communicate with Gaslighters 25

Where do people experience gaslighting? 31

How to deal with gaslighting—and heal its effects ... 37

GREENLIGHTING **44**

What is greenlighting? *44*

How to experience greenlighting *46*

Is Gaslighting Intentional? *46*

How to Break Up With a Gaslighter *58*

GASLIGHTING CHILDREN 65

What Does It Look Like? *65*

Dealing With Gaslighting *75*

TRUSTING YOURSELF 86

How to Learn to Trust Yourself *86*

You Can Heal Stronger *90*

INTRODUCTION

Gaslighting is a dangerous form of abuse precisely because it's so hard to spot. It distorts the very thing we hold most dear: our perception of reality.

A common tactic of emotional and physical abuse, gaslighting received its name from a 1938 British play and subsequent film, Gas Light. A chilling mystery, the play features a man who, in a plot to get his wife committed to an "insane asylum" so he can steal her precious jewels, slowly convinces her that she's losing touch with reality. Every time the husband turns the light on in the couple's attic to search for the jewels, the gas lights in the rest of the house dim. But when the wife calls him out on the deception, he convinces her that the lights didn't dim at all, and that in fact she is losing touch with reality.

"Gaslighting is the basic act of manipulating someone by psychological means into questioning their thoughts, beliefs, or actions."

It's a common tactic in emotionally and physically abusive relationships, and it's a betrayal of basic trust.

If you've been gaslit, the experience has likely been difficult to get over. But know it's possible to take back your reality. There are common signs of gaslighting that you can use to spot this harmful behavior. As you heal, you can learn ways to guard your own sense of reality and validate yourself, so that no matter what people around you do or say, you'll always have your own back.

GASLIGHTING

What Is Gaslighting?

Gaslighting is a form of manipulation that occurs in abusive relationships. It is an insidious, and sometimes covert, type of emotional abuse where the bully or abuser makes the target question their judgments and reality. Ultimately, the victim of gaslighting starts to wonder if they are going crazy.

Gaslighting primarily occurs in dating and married relationships. But it is not uncommon for it to occur in controlling friendships or among family members as well.

Toxic people use this type of manipulation to exert power over others in order to manipulate friends, family members, and sometimes even co-workers.

Why is Gaslighting so Terrible?

In case it is not obvious, gaslighting is terrible because it is a planned, plotted, and intentional abusive behavior on the part of a cheater or emotional abuser. A cheater who is gaslighting his or her betrayed spouse is knowingly abusing his or her spouse. A cheater knowingly uses this form of abuse to keep total control of a betrayed spouse and life after D-Day.

A gaslighter knows that both cheating and gaslighting is wrong, but they do it to intentionally wear down their spouse and take away a betrayed spouse's confidence. Gaslighting will create an invisible cage around a victim. The victim could leave the metaphorical cage at any point, but they will be a prisoner of their own mind and they will see no other options but to stay. In a sense, they have been brainwashed to feel as if staying in an abusive marriage is the only option and as if they will fail if they leave their marriage.

I am aware of people in my personal (off-line) circles who have enough money to leave a marriage and who would have the ability to live the life most people dream of. But, their spouse gaslights them so often, that they cannot even imagine life on the outside.

Tactics Used in Gaslighting

Gaslighting is a technique that undermines your entire perception of reality. When someone is gaslighting you, you often second-guess yourself, your memories and your perceptions. After communicating with the person gaslighting you, you are left feeling dazed and wondering what is wrong with you. Tactics like these can confuse you and cause you to question your sanity.

- Lying to You

People who engage in gaslighting are habitual and pathological liars. They will blatantly lie to your face and never back down or change their stories, even when you call them out or provide proof of their deception. Lying is the cornerstone of their destructive behavior. Even when you know they are lying, they can be very convincing. In the end, you start to second-guess yourself.

- Discrediting You to Others

Gaslighters spread rumors and gossip about you to others. They may pretend to be worried about you while subtly telling others that you seem emotionally unstable or crazy.

Unfortunately, this tactic can be extremely effective and many people may side with the abuser or bully without knowing the full story. Additionally, the gaslighter may lie to you and tell you that other people think you are crazy. These people may never say a bad thing about you, but the gaslighter will make every attempt to get you to believe they do.

- Deflecting Blame

When you ask a gaslighter a question or call them out for something they did or said, they may change the subject by asking a question instead of responding to the issue at hand. They may blatantly lie about the situation by saying something like: "You're making things up. That never happened."

- Minimizing Your Thoughts and Feelings

Trivializing your emotions allows the gaslighter to gain power over you. They might make statements like: "Calm down," "You're overreacting," or "Why are you so sensitive?" All of these statements minimize how you are feeling or what you are thinking and communicate that you are wrong.

When you deal with someone who never acknowledges your thoughts, your feelings or your beliefs, you will begin to question them yourself. What's more, you never feel validated or understood, which can be extremely difficult to cope with.

- Shifting Blame to You

Blame-shifting is a common tactic of gaslighters. Every discussion you have is somehow twisted to where you are to blame for something that has occurred. Even when you try to discuss how their behavior makes you feel, they are able to twist the conversation and end up blaming you.

In other words, they manipulate the situation in such a way that you end up believing that you are the cause of their bad behavior. They claim that if only you behaved differently, they would not treat you the way that they do.

- Denying Wrongdoing

Bullies and abusers are notorious for denying that they did anything wrong. They do this in order to avoid taking responsibility for their poor choices. But it also leaves the victim of gaslighting confused and frustrated because there is no acknowledgment of the pain they have caused. This also makes it very hard for the victim to move on or to heal from the bullying or abusiveness.

- Using Compassionate Words as a Weapon

Sometimes when called out or questioned, a gaslighter will use kind and loving words to try to smooth over the situation. They might say something like "You know how much I love you. I would never hurt you on purpose."

These words are what you want to hear, but they are not authentic, especially if the same behavior is repeated.

When you are dealing with someone who uses gaslighting as a manipulation tool, pay close attention to their actions, not their words. Is this person truly loving, or are they only saying loving things?

- Twisting and Reframing Conversations

Gaslighters typically use this tactic when you are discussing something that happened in the past. For instance, if your partner shoved you against the wall and you are discussing it later, they may twist the story in their favor. They may say you stumbled and they tried to steady you, which in turn caused you to fall into the wall.

When stories and memories are constantly retold in the gaslighter's favor, you may begin to doubt your memory of what happened. This is exactly the goal.

Signs You Are a Victim of Gaslighting

Being subject to gaslighting can cause anxiety and depression. It also has been linked to panic attacks and nervous breakdowns. For this reason, it is important to recognize when you are being gaslighted. Ask yourself if any of the following statements ring true.

• You doubt your feelings and reality. You try to convince yourself that the treatment you receive is not that bad, or that you are too sensitive.

• You doubt your judgment and perceptions. You are afraid of speaking up or expressing your emotions. You have learned that sharing your opinion usually makes you feel worse in the end. So you stay silent instead.

• You feel vulnerable and insecure. As a result, you often feel like you "walk on eggshells" around your partner/friend/family member. You feel on edge and lack self-esteem.

- You feel alone and powerless. You are convinced that everyone around you thinks you are strange, crazy or unstable, just like your partner/friend/family member says you are. This makes you feel trapped and isolated.

- You feel stupid and crazy. Your partner/friend/family member's words make you feel like you are wrong, inadequate, or insane. Sometimes you even find yourself repeating these statements to yourself.

- You are disappointed in yourself and who you have become. For instance, you feel like you are weak and passive and that you used to be stronger and more assertive.

- You feel confused. Your partner/friend/family member's behavior confuses you—with actions that appear like Dr. Jekyll and Mr. Hyde.

- You worry that you are too sensitive. Your partner/friend/family member minimizes hurtful behaviors or words by saying "I was just joking" or "You are too sensitive."

- You have a sense of impending doom. You feel like something terrible is about to happen when you are around your partner/friend/family member. This may include feeling threatened and on edge without knowing why.

- You spend a lot of time apologizing. You feel the need to apologize all the time for what you do or who you are.

- You feel inadequate. You feel like you are never "good enough." You try to live up to the expectations and demands of others, even if they are unreasonable.

- You second-guess yourself. You frequently wonder if you accurately remember the details of past events. You may have even stopped trying to share what you remember for fear that it is wrong.

- You assume others are disappointed in you. You apologize all the time for what you do or who you are, assuming people are disappointed in you or that you have somehow made a mistake.

- You wonder what's wrong with you. You wonder if there's something fundamentally wrong with you. In other words, you worry that you might truly be crazy, neurotic, or "losing it."

- You struggle to make decisions, because you distrust yourself. You would rather allow your partner/friend/family member to make decisions for you, or avoid decision-making altogether.

RECOGNIZING AND RESPONDING TO GASLIGHTING

What to Do About It

It is imperative that you are alert to the idea that a cheater will most likely be gaslighting you. Here is what is recommended:

• Send a short email to yourself – in a password protected account – describing each incident

• Create a password protected journal detailing your thoughts

• Tell trusted friends and family members that you believe your spouse is playing "mind games." Ask them to serve as reality-checkers for you.

• Do NOT isolate yourself, even if you feel like curling up into a ball and laying in bed

- Join an online support group such as "Out of the Fog."

- Create an exit strategy if your gaslighter becomes verbally aggressive.

- Become a volunteer at a place that you feel passionate about and make friends with like-minded people. If you do not feel up to facing people, there are thousands and dogs and cats that could use your care via the Humane Society of the United States. Local branches need someone to walk dogs and play with cats. They also need photographers to take photos of pets and create adoption profiles for them.

- Remind yourself that no matter how much it hurts, you must NOT take in the message of a gaslighter.

- Reframe the way you view a gaslighter. If you think about it, people who use gaslighting as a strategy are often very pathetic human beings who have poor self-control, poor self-regulation, and who must project their faults onto others. However, do not have sympathy for them because they are trying to victimize you.

- If a gaslighter cannot stop twisting your reality, buy a body camera for $20 and tell the gaslighter you will be wearing it all the time to record and review conversations. Tell the gas-lighter that you will record all interactions and then you will bring these recorded interactions to a marriage and family therapist. Gaslighters thrive when they can hide; if you record all interactions and show them to a professional, a gaslighter will know the game is over.

- Avoid people who reinforce the narrative of a gaslighter. For example, a cheater/gaslighter might say: "If you gained/lost 20 pounds I would not have cheated." If you confide this in a friend or family member and they say, "He has a point," that person is not someone you can trust to help you stay in factual reality. Remember, cheating is a choice. There is nothing you can do to cause someone cheat on you since this behavior comes from within them.

A word recognizing and responding to gaslighting from Psych Central:

- Recognize the pattern of undermining behavior. Gaslighting only works when a victim isn't aware of what's going on. Once you become alert to the pattern, it will not affect you as much. You may be able to say to yourself, "Here we go again" and shrug it off.

- Keep in mind that the gaslighting isn't about you. It's about the gaslighter's need for control and power. Often the gaslighter is a very insecure human being. In order to feel "equal", they need to feel superior. In order to feel safe, they need to feel they have the upper hand. They have few other coping skills or other ways to negotiate differences. That doesn't excuse the behavior. But knowing that may help you take it less personally while you decide whether to maintain the relationship.

- Be aware that you are unlikely to be able to change the gaslighter – at least on your own. Gaslighting behavior is the only way gaslighters know to manage their world. For that reason, they are not likely to respond to rational appeals to change. It usually requires intensive therapy, done willingly, for a gaslighter to give it up.

- Rethink whether the relationship is worth putting up with the constant attempts to chip away at your self-esteem. If the gaslighter is your boss or supervisor, start looking for another job. If the person is a family member or friend, consider how to put some distance between you. If it's a significant other and you want to preserve the relationship, you will probably need to insist on couple's counseling.

- Develop your own support system. You need other people in your life who can confirm your reality and worth. Gaslighters often try to isolate their victims in order to stay in control. They often further manipulate their victims by repeatedly telling them that they are the only person who really loves and understands them. Don't buy it. Spend time with friends and family. Check out your perceptions by talking to other people who witnessed what the gaslighter is calling into question.

- Work on rebuilding your self-esteem. Remind yourself that you are a loveable and capable person, regardless of the opinion of the gaslighter. Help yourself regain perspective by reminding yourself of other times in your life when you have felt grounded, sane, and generally good about yourself. It may be helpful to keep a private journal in which you document events that the gaslighter is likely to contest. Record positive experiences and affirmations of your own worth as well.

• Get professional help if you need it. Victims often lose confidence in their own thoughts and feelings and find themselves nervously double-checking themselves on a regular basis. Sometimes they sink into the depressive feelings of being helpless and hopeless. If you recognize yourself in this paragraph, you will probably need professional help to dig your way back out of the devastating effects of gaslighting. A therapist can offer you practical advice and support to help you recover."

How to Communicate with Gaslighters

While the Psych Central article provides excellent insight into the mind of the cheating gaslighter and some things for you to do, I believe it's important to have some key phrases to interrupt the cycle of gaslighting. Cheaters who are gaslighting will be solely focused on pointing our your flaws. They will do so to assuage their guilt. But, they will also do so in hope that you don't question their affair.

Cheaters who gaslight will often spray "word bullets" at you and they will do it so quickly that you cannot keep track. They will do this to confuse you and cause you to lose your equilibrium. The phrases below are ONLY to be used to interrupt an incident of gaslighting. If they are used within the wrong context, they could cause you to be further emotionally abused. The goal is to get a gaslighter to stop spraying "word bullets" at you and to question their reality.

Once you question their reality, you can state factual behaviors and events that you do that are contrary to what they are saying. These are a tactic to interrupt gaslighting and I do NOT in any way encourage emotional abuse. Also, if your gas-lighter wants to keep blame-shifting, keep asking them for examples. Then, be very confident, calm, and factual to show them that what they are saying is not true.

Of course, some of these phrases may cause a gaslighter to huff off. Let them be.

I would also recommend carrying your phone or a recording device with you when you ask these questions.

These questions are NOT tactics to help you relate to an abusive spouse; they are suggestions on how to interrupt someone who is actively gas-lighting you. If you want tactics on how to relate to an abusive spouse, you are on the wrong path. You don't relate to abusive spouses; you serve concrete consequences.

When you use these phrases, move your body in a way to have an open stance, make direct eye contact, and assume very assertive body language when a cheater is gaslighting you. You must establish yourself as at least an equal using body language. Once you have done that, here are some examples of key phrases to use to interrupt a gaslighter:

- Can you explain to me what you mean by (fill in the blank)?

- What factual information do you have that causes you to believe (fill in the blank)?

- Can you describe (fill in the blank) in concrete terms? We all know that nothing is "always or never." Can you be more specific?

- It's easy to see that I have done something to upset you; can you tell me more about it?

- How would you feel if I were telling you what you are telling me now?

- How would you feel if I called you a (fill in the blank?)

- How would you like to be treated? Can be specific about things I can do to make you happy?

- How can I communicate in ways that are better?

- Give me concrete steps that I need to take to improve. Please walk me through this step-by-step process, so that I can understand your viewpoint. (Then tell them it's a two-way street and tell them things they must stop doing.)

- Can you please make a list of behaviors that you would like for me to display and behaviors that you do not want me to display? It would be great if you could get started on that list now so that I can review it as soon as possible. I will post it on the refrigerator for constant reference. I will also make a list for you.

- Can you describe how you perceive me and can you give me factual behaviors that I do everyday that reinforce your perception of me?

- I am always happy to discuss things constructively and it would be great if you lowered your voice.

- Now is not the time to discuss (fill in the blank) so let's discuss this after (such and such a time).

- You are projecting your own behaviors on to me and I need you to stop now.

- Uh huh. Oh I see. Got it. Okay. Yeah. I was thinking of doing (fill in the blank) on Saturday. Would this interest you?

Finally, there will be times that you need to tell a gaslighter that the conversation is heading nowhere good. Tell the gaslighter that you will get in your car and take a drive for 20 minutes so that each of you have time to clear your head. Or, ask the gaslighter if he or she would like to have some alone time in his or her office/car.

Where do people experience gaslighting?

Gaslighting can occur in different settings where we interact with other people, for instance, in the family, within intimate relationships, or in the workplace.

Let's look at these:

Family

Children are particularly susceptible to gaslighting, as science writer Peg Streep explains:

"The parent-child relationship isn't one of equals—in fact, it's terrifically lopsided. All of the power is vested in the parent and while it's a thought that might make you cringe, where there's power, there's also the potential abuse of power."

She goes on to explain that while it takes work to gaslight adult,

"There's not much work involved making a love-deprived and insecure child doubt his or her reality."

Comedian Randy Rainbow gives an example of what it feels like to grow up with someone prone to gaslighting:

"My father was a textbook narcissist. If he didn't like the narrative he'd start gaslighting you. He threatened the democracy of our family."

Couples

As Lachlan Brown describes, when compared to a parent-child or boss-employee relationship, in "a romantic partnership, gaslighting can be more difficult to observe and admit, as there is an assumed equal power dynamic between two partners."

That doesn't make it uncommon. For instance, according to psychotherapist Stephanie Sarkis, gaslighting is present in about 30–40% of the couples she treats (where this is more commonly represented) and is just as likely to be done by men as women.

Work

Based on my observations, I assume that gaslighting and general toxic behavior in the workplace happens more often than we might think.

As a career coach, it's not uncommon for me to have clients describe situations that amount to gaslighting in the workplace.

Similarly, a Twitter poll by HR software and services provider MHR found that 58% of respondents have experienced what they consider to be gaslighting during their working lives.

Their employee engagement expert, Chris Kerridge, describes gaslighting in the workplace as follows:

"Unlike bullying, which is very clear and obvious, gaslighting is a very subtle form of manipulation which can destroy a victim's confidence, leave them feeling extremely vulnerable and, in some cases, force them to quit their jobs. In many cases it can be so subtle that some people may not even know it's happening until they stop and think about it, which is perhaps why it happens so frequently."

This is in alignment with Sarkis' observation that gaslighting is "underreported in the workplace, because gaslighters who are particularly adept at manipulation may make the victim feel as if it was all his or her fault."

Even if you're lucky enough to not experience this dynamic in your personal relationships or at work, it probably still impacts your life. That's because gaslighting also extends to other levels.

Can gaslighting occur outside of personal relationships?

Yes, gaslighting isn't limited to personal relationships. It can also happen in a more widespread form, for instance, if an organization or entity tried to manipulate everyone's experience.

This excerpt from George Orwell's novel 1984 would be a classic example of gaslighting in real life:

"The Party told you to reject the evidence of your eyes and ears. It was their final, most essential command."

As Sarkis remarks in an article:

"Gaslighting behavior has always been present in history, to a degree. It is par for the course whenever a person or entity wants to exert as much control as possible over others. But we haven't seen this level of gaslighting since the Axis powers of World War II."

In his 2008 book "State of Confusion: Political Manipulation and the Assault on the American Mind," psychologist Bryan Welch makes the point that gaslighting isn't anything new:

"To say gaslighting was started by the Bushes, Lee Atwater, Karl Rove, Fox News, or any other extant group is not simply wrong, it also misses an important point. Gaslighting comes directly from blending modern communications, marketing, and advertising techniques with long-standing methods of propaganda. They were simply waiting to be discovered by those with sufficient ambition and psychological makeup to use them."

Given how frequent gaslighting is in all our lives—whether or not you've ever personally experienced it—we must get good at recognizing this dynamic and learning how to deal with it.

This will make us more resilient and harder to manipulate.

How to deal with gaslighting—and heal its effects

To find out how to deal with and heal the effects of gaslighting, let's turn our attention to a man we don't know a lot about, the fabulist Phaedrus who lived in the 1st century CE.

According to Phaedrus:

"Gentleness is the antidote for cruelty."

While Phaedrus doesn't state this specifically, his choice of antidote is based on a wider-reaching principle that I would call the "Exact Opposite Principle":

The remedy for a negative emotional influence is its exact opposite.

Gentleness is the exact opposite of cruelty—which is why it can be its antidote.

So, let's apply this newfound principle to gaslighting, which is exposure to people who make one question one's reality in ways that are hard to detect.

As you can see, there are 3 components of gaslighting each of which needs its own antidote:

• Hard to detect (antidote: awareness of the telltale signs of gaslighting),

• Exposure to gaslighters (antidote: avoidance of gaslighters),

• Doubts about one's reality (antidote: confirmation of one's reality).

Let's explore what each of them looks like:

Antidote 1: increasing awareness of gaslighting

Sharing resources about gaslighting with people who may be subject to it is helpful because it can make them aware of what is indeed happening.

For instance, imagine if Bella had come across a newspaper article describing this dynamic early on. It would have made it easier for her to realize that her perception was accurate all along.

And what a relief that could be!

However, even though it's helpful to raise awareness about the dynamics of gaslighting, by itself it's not enough.

Which brings us to the other two antidotes.

Antidote 2: limiting exposure to gaslighters

"Letting go of toxic people in your life is a big step in loving yourself."

Like many issues, the antidote to gaslighting has an external and an internal component.

On the external level, the most obvious solution is to limit contact with people who engage in gaslighting as much as possible.

You don't need to spend time with a friend, acquaintance, or family member who makes you feel bad. While handling your closest relationships might be more complicated for logistical reasons, you can still strive to limit the time you spend with an immediate family member who gaslights you.

The same advice applies to workplace gaslighting. If it's not possible to avoid or handle toxic people at work, you might want to consider changing your job.

I would also recommend that you stop reading the news so much.

Manipulative behaviors tend to lose their power over you the less you get exposed to them. This also gives you space and safety to explore how you feel and get back to your own equilibrium.

Antidote 3: confirmation of one's reality

"As soon as you trust yourself, you will know how to live."

One of the main things gaslighting does is to make people doubt their own experiences. That's why it is necessary to get back to a place of trusting one's own reality.

Even in healthy relationships, fully trusting our own experiences can be challenging at times. That is because, for all the talk about individualism, humans have been communal beings throughout most of our history—depending on others for our very survival.

And as communal beings, there is a way in which we frame our reality by considering how those around us are acting and how they are perceiving the world.

When people get manipulated or otherwise hurt in relationships, the damage caused needs to be repaired where it originated—in relationships.

One extremely helpful approach for healing relationship wounds and getting to a place where one trusts one's own experience is a little-known spiritual practice called greenlighting.

Let's explore this in more depth.

GREENLIGHTING

What is greenlighting?

Greenlighting is a form of profound compassion and radical acceptance for your inner experiences or the experiences of someone else.

As such, it differs radically from the idea of "fixing" ourselves or somebody else—thinking that something needs to be "fixed" assumes that it is broken.

Greenlighting is something I use a lot in my coaching but because few people are familiar with this specific meaning of the term, I instead describe it as "compassionate self-understanding" (which is close enough).

However, one thing that is special about the term greenlighting is that it has a more active undertone than words such as "self-understanding" or "acceptance" etc.

In fact, to me greenlighting is the opposite of passive complacency.

As a term borrowed from the film industry, it refers to the stage where a project is given permission to go ahead, which allows it to move out of the development stage. That a project receives the "green light" doesn't mean that it's already a polished and finished movie that can be shown on the screen.

Greenlighting involves treating your experience of life like that movie project—something that is simultaneously okay just as it is, while also being in flux and having a lot of potential for further development.

It is a way of constantly saying, "Yes!" to all of whom we are, to our entire past, current, and emerging being.

In short, it is the exact opposite of gaslighting.

As such, greenlighting is the perfect antidote for healing it.

How to experience greenlighting

"Relationships are like traffic lights. And I just have this theory that I can only exist in a relationship if it's a green light."

There are two ways in which we can experience greenlighting: by another person or by ourselves.

Typically, we first need to receive this type of holding and support from somebody else before we can more deeply give it to ourselves. This might require finding the right person(s) to receive greenlighting from.

Is Gaslighting Intentional?

One might wonder: is all gaslighting intentional? After all, we've all had experiences where we've inadvertently invalidated someone's experience without meaning to. Perhaps we lacked enough information about the matter. Maybe we were defensive about being right. Or, we just didn't agree with their "interpretation" of events. Everyday gaslighting may occur due to human error – but that does not negate the danger of gaslighting when it is used to emotionally terrorize someone.

In the context of an abusive relationship, gaslighting is used to deliberately undercut the victim's reality and make him or her more malleable to mistreatment. "Are Gaslighters Aware of What They Do?" not all gaslighters engage in it intentionally, but those who are cult leaders, dictators and malignant narcissists most certainly do so with an agenda in mind.

The goal is to make the victim or victims question their own reality and depend on the gaslighter. In the case of a person who has a personality disorder such as antisocial personality disorder, they are born with an insatiable need to control others.

Gaslighting allows perpetrators to evade accountability for their actions, to deflect responsibility and exercise their control over their partners with alarming ease.

Beliefs, after all, are immensely powerful. They have the power to create division, build or destroy nations, end or start wars. To mold the beliefs of an unsuspecting target to suit your own agendas is to essentially control their behavior and even potentially change their life-course trajectory. If narcissistic Calvin decides he wants to wreak havoc over his girlfriend Brianna's reality, all he has to do is to convince her that she cannot trust herself or her instincts – especially about the abuse she is experiencing.

Are You Being Gaslighted at Work?

Here's What to Do About This Dangerous Form of Abuse.

Gaslighters create their own reality. Within this twisted world, they're always right, and their opponent—anyone they decide they want to dominate, basically—is wrong, misguided, and uninformed. The goal of a gaslighter is to deceive and obfuscate to gain power over you. Dating a gaslighter is challenging. But so too is having one as your supervisor or coworker.

This form of workplace harassment may be more common than you think. "Gaslighting and other forms of harassment are underreported in the workplace, because gaslighters who are particularly adept at manipulation may make the victim feel as if it was all his or her fault," says Stephanie Sarkis, PhD, author of Gaslighting:

Recognize Manipulative and Emotionally Abusive People—and Break Free.

Gaslighters are often very smart. Their intellect, combined with their inability to handle negative feedback, means they often assume positions of authority in the workplace. More often than not, they'll either be an entrepreneur or in some position of power—that's where they're much more comfortable.

As there are often hierarchies of authority and power differentials in the workplace, this context provides the ideal manipulative leverage for gaslighters.

For example, an individual who makes their coworker feel unskilled and mentally off may do so to appear competent in the eyes of the supervisor. Sarkis describes some workplace gaslighting behaviors such as:

- Stealing credit for another's work

- Throwing coworkers under the bus

- Pitting coworkers against each other

- Giving undeserved negative reviews

- Harassing or intimidating coworkers

- Making up stories to get coworkers fired

- Threatening lawsuits

Like in other contexts, gaslighting in the workplace results in various problems for victims, such as anxiety, exhaustion, powerlessness, and the doubting of their perceptions.

Ultimately, narcissistic workplace behaviors such as those noted above are highly detrimental, often leaving victims apprehensive about going to work each day, feeling alienated from others, experiencing immune system weakness, unhappy and dissatisfied at work, and experiencing high rates of work absences.

As workplace gaslighting has the potential to cause a high level of damage at both an individual and organizational level, both employers and staff need to recognize warning signs and take action as soon as possible.

Working for a boss with gaslighting tendencies or having a gaslighting coworker with authority over you can diminish your confidence and leave you feeling paranoid and off-kilter—not just during work hours but around the clock, so the abuse cuts into your personal life. Getting a new job is an option, but it's not your only recourse. Here's what experts recommend.

- Make sure it really is gaslighting

A tough manager who is hard to please is one thing; they might quibble with a report you turned in but then give you the feedback and time to get it right. A manager who is a gaslighter is another, and there's a way to tell the difference.

A gaslighter doesn't really want you to succeed at all and will sabotage your efforts. They might change due dates and deadlines in the middle of a project, leaving you pulling all nighters to get it done. They might undermine your efforts with comments about how you don't know what your doing...making you doubt your own expertise.

Extreme gaslighters might even say disparaging things or touch you inappropriately, then deny it happened, claim it was an accident, or call you a liar when you confront them. Remember, gaslighters try to bend reality to make their version of events the only true one. They cross lines most of us wouldn't, which is how they get away with their harassment.

Gaslighters are going to communicate that they know more, that you don't know what you're talking about, and that you're confused and uninformed.

- Document everything

Once you're sure it really is gaslighting, start documenting every email, memo, and other evidence proving what's going on. Don't trust your memory. Keep a record of every interaction where gaslighting occurs, including dates and times, says Sarkis. "Do not keep this information on a work-issued device, as your company may have access to that information and will take the device upon you quitting," she advises.

Tracking the gaslighting accomplishes two important goals. First, it helps you confirm to yourself the severity of the situation. In some cases, you may be able to live with your supervisor's behavior or develop workarounds that allow you to still do your job. If not, documentation is also invaluable if you decide to get higher ups or human resources involved.

A verbal account isn't compelling to HR folks and high-level supervisors, and it also tends to give your boss an advantage. Gaslighters will talk their way out of a bag. Digital or paper proof, however, lays out your case.

- Ask colleagues if it's happening to them, too

Sometimes a gaslighter at work will focus their abuse on one employee. But often they see many people in their path to power, and they gaslight them as well. So do a little intel. How does your boss interact with the other people on your team? If coworkers say that they also receive similar treatment, ask them if they're willing to document the gaslighting behavior they have to deal with. That way, it won't be just you making a complaint. Remember, there's strength in numbers.

- Schedule a one-on-one with the gaslighter

After reviewing all your evidence, schedule time to meet with your boss. Be direct and firm, sharing how you feel and asking how you two can form a better working relationship. Try to avoid accusations and a confrontational tone, because if there's one thing that sets of a gaslighter, it's critical, negative feedback.

If they truly have gaslighting tendencies, they're probably not going to hear you and will throw that back at you that whatever you tell them is really your fault.

Document your conversation as well, even via handwritten notes. It's possible, although unlikely, that your conversation will lead to changed behavior. Mostly, this interaction is necessary office politics, says Gatter. When you meet with the gaslighter's supervisor or human resources, you'll be able to show that you tried to address the problem on your own.

- Go to HR or other higher-ups

Check your employee manual to see if your office has a policy on handling complaints about a manager. If there is no official policy, reach out to HR or the gaslighter's supervisor to share your experience.

You can't necessarily predict how the company will respond. A best-case scenario would result in your manager backing off, and you resume doing your job the way you always did (and regain your mental health as well). The company could opt to transfer you so you have a different manager. Unfortunately, it's also possible that the company won't support you.

In that case, it may make the most sense to seek out another job rather than return to the same situation and endure the anxiety, depression, and other mental anguish caused by a gaslighter. It's not fair that you need to leave, but what is it costing you to stay. If you find yourself in this position, weigh your options carefully. The toll a gaslighter takes on your health may justify handing in your resignation.

How to Break Up With a Gaslighter

Ending any romantic relationship is never easy. But perhaps the hardest breakup of all is with a gaslighter—

someone who uses lies and deception to make you doubt reality and thus gain power over you (aka, gaslighting).

The reason it's so tricky is simple. Typically, gaslighters do not want to break up. In most cases, they want to stay in the relationship and keep it on their terms.

When gaslighters are faced with a breakup conversation, they'll turn to their familiar tactics: deceit, distortion of reality, and defensive attacks. Tell a gaslighter why you want to part ways, and the response could be a denial of an event happening, claims of being misinterpreted, or calling you names, like overly sensitive or crazy.

Making this breakup even more difficult is that after being involved with a gaslighter, your confidence and self-worth may be particularly fragile. Gaslighters get you in the habit of questioning your own reality, which means you're trained to wonder if your reasons for breaking up are valid. The more you second-guess your decision, the less likely you'll follow through.

But since breaking free of the emotional abuse and dysfunction gaslighters cause is imperative, it's something you have to do. To help, we asked experts for the exact steps to take and problems to anticipate.

- Break up in one quick conversation

One key to a successful split with a gaslighter is to make it fast, ideally in a single conversation. Tell them it's not working and the relationship is over, and say it in a straightforward, calm, and direct voice. It can't hurt to enlist a friend to act out the breakup convo with you, so you know exactly what you want to say. Try to avoid language that offers any wiggle room the gaslighter will use to try to change your mind.

- Don't believe promises to change

As soon as you say the relationship is done, your former partner will try to win you back. Expect instant apologies and promises that things will be different, says Florida-based therapist Stephanie Sarkis, PhD, author of Gaslighting: Recognize Manipulative and Emotionally Abusive People—and Break Free. Their words will sound sincere, and part of you might want to believe them. Don't. It's all part of the manipulation. If you do cave, the unhealthy relationship dynamic will return and perhaps get worse, says Sarkis.

- End all communication

Because gaslighters are so bent on trying to win you back, both Weiler and Sarkis recommend ceasing communication once you've officially ended things.

"Block their phone numbers and emails. Do not answer any calls from unknown numbers," advises Sarkis.

A gaslighter may attempt to communicate with you through social media, so make sure you've blocked them from all your accounts. They will also try to enlist mutual friends in their effort to get back together. Sarkis calls these emissaries "flying monkeys," after the characters in The Wizard of Oz. "Tell these flying monkeys that you will not be discussing the gaslighter with them, and if the gaslighter is brought up again, you will need to walk away from the conversation," she says.

- Ask friends to remind you how bad things were

Even when you know breaking up was for the best, you still might be grieving the end of a relationship that at one point seemed so promising. This is when leaning on loved ones comes in, says Weiler. When thoughts of giving the gaslighter a second chance creep into your head, your support network will remind you of what it was like dating someone who lied and deceived you—and that you deserve better.

If friends and family aren't on hand, counseling can really help, particularly group therapy. "Group therapy can be great because it helps you realize that you are not the only one who has been through a relationship like this," says Sarkis.

• Make a list—and check it in moments of doubt

A simple list can be a helpful tool after a break up, says Weiler. Write out all the times you felt gaslighted during the relationship. Whenever you have doubts about just how toxic the relationship was, or when your ex reaches once again with hopes of reconciling (and they will; gaslighters don't give up easily), read through it. The point is to remind you that the relationship was unhealthy and unworkable, and to reaffirm your commitment to staying away from them forever.

GASLIGHTING CHILDREN

What Does It Look Like?

Questions about gaslightingWith their apparent vulnerability and powerlessness, children also may be targets of gaslighting tactics within the family system.

Many of the ways in which parents gaslight their kids are consistent with tactics used toward adults, such as ridicule; making them feel inadequate, worthless, or unloved; and convincing them that they are not normal.

Drawn from articles by McCleod (2018) and Sarkis (2018), below are 17 examples of how child gaslighting and coercive control by parents may appear:

- Within dysfunctional or abusive households, children may be blamed for the chaos.

- Violence against other members of the family may be used as a way to manipulate the child.

- Children may be restricted from social activities or isolated from friends as a way of exercising control while denying opportunities for supportive relationships.

- Unrealistic homework and chore expectations may be used as a way of controlling children's time and participation in positive activities.

- Parents may create resentment and tension between siblings by pitting them against each other such as by assigning one child with a positive label and the other child with one that is degrading. Phrases such as "Why can't you be more like your brother?" also enhance resentment.

- Excessive parental supervision and monitoring (perhaps with the use of spyware) may be used to demean the child's privacy and sense of autonomy.

- Children may be prohibited from expressing their feelings or opinions.

- Children may be deprived of social services such as counseling.

- Children may be forbidden from having friends in the home, thereby precluding others from seeing what's going on in the family.

- Parents may micromanage children's schoolwork, perhaps destroying it and making them start over.

- Children may be deprived of essential resources such as certain foods or technology.

- Parents may make fun of children or engage in destructive teasing.

- Parents may enforce excessive rules.

- Parents may show a lack of regard for children's developmental periods.

- Parents may control movement within the home.

- Parents may demand respect from children without reciprocating it.

- Parents may habitually break promises.

The above dysfunctional parenting practices are common ways for gaslighters to enhance their manipulative control over children. Additionally, parental alienation, in which one parent turns a child against the other (often following divorce) as a way of punishing the other parent, is another type of parental gaslighting that is exceptionally hurtful to children.

Importantly, along with being highly detrimental to kids, gaslighting behaviors are frequently passed down to the next generation. Children raised by gaslighters will often apply these same tactics in their own relationships, a behavior that is referred to by Sarkis as 'fleas,' meaning 'lie down with dogs, and you will end up with fleas.'

It is thus imperative to break the cycle of gaslighting behavior before it extends its destructive grasp toward more potential victims.

The Role of Gaslighting in Sexual Addiction

Gaslighting is a form of psychological abuse in which false information is presented, usually repeatedly, as true, causing the victim to doubt his or her judgment, sense of reality and even sanity. The term derives from the 1938 stage play, Gaslight, and a pair of eponymous 1940s film adaptations. The most well-known of these was released in 1944, starring Charles Boyer and Ingrid Bergman. In it, Boyer's character convinces his wife (played by Bergman) that she's imagining the occasional dimming of their home's gas lights. (The lights dim whenever he is in the attic, searching for his wife's deceased aunt's jewels, which he hopes to steal.) Over time, his persistent lies cause Bergman's character to question her sanity.

Admittedly, the plot of Gaslight is outlandish, but the concept of denying a person's intuitive sense of reality is actually a common form of modern-day abuse and manipulation. In fact, addicts engage in this type of behavior relatively often as a way of manipulating their loved ones into supporting (or ignoring) their addiction. Sex addicts are no exception. They often lie to their spouses/partners for years, insisting that they really did need to stay late at work, that they're not being emotionally distant, that they're not cheating and if it seems like they are it's because the cheated-on partner is being paranoid and unfair. Over time, in the face of consistent, persistent and insistent lies, betrayed spouses can lose faith in their intuition and sense of reality, eventually blaming themselves for what they are thinking and feeling about their relationship.

The really frightening thing about gaslighting is that even emotionally healthy people are vulnerable to it, mostly because it tends to build slowly and gradually. In this respect, gaslighting victims are like a frog placed in a pot of warm water that is then set to boil. The temperature rises slowly, almost imperceptibly, and because of that the frog never suspects it's being cooked. In similar fashion, with gaslighting the lies usually start out as relatively minor and easily believable. Over time, as the betrayed partner begins to doubt his/her perceptions of reality, the fabrications may become outlandish, but by then the victim's ability to discern the truth about his or her relationship is greatly diminished.

Interestingly, after the truth about sex addiction and serial cheating is uncovered, it is usually the addict's gaslighting (the lies and deceit) that causes the most pain. In other words, with sexual addiction it's not any specific sexual act that does the most damage; instead, it's the ongoing betrayal of relationship trust that hurts the most. Much of this pain derives from the fact that this mistreatment has been perpetrated by a loved one in the context of a relationship that has other, more positive elements. The emotional/psychological effects of sex addiction and gaslighting can be quite severe. One study looking at the wives of male sex addicts found that upon learning about their husbands' repeated infidelity, many of these women experienced acute stress and anxiety symptoms characteristic of PTSD (post-traumatic stress disorder).[ii] In case you don't know, PTSD is a very serious psychological disorder with potentially disastrous long-term effects. This is the sort of abuse that sex addicts intentionally perpetrate on their loved ones!

Sadly, the cheated-on spouses and partners of sex addicts often resent the suggestion that they might want to seek help with their feelings about and responses to the betrayal they've experienced. For most of these folks, the automatic (and perfectly natural) response is assigning blame to the addict. After all, the addict is the person who did something wrong. Nevertheless, betrayed spouses, especially if they have also been victimized by gaslighting, usually do benefit from therapeutic assistance. At the very least, therapy provides much-needed validation of their feelings, empathy for how their life has been thrown into chaos by the addict, help in processing the shame of being cheated on and believing the addict's (now obvious) lies and education and support for moving forward.

Sometimes the betrayed partners of sex addicts decide the violation they've experienced is greater than their desire to continue the relationship. For them, trust is too badly damaged and cannot be restored, so ending things is the best course of action. These individuals may still benefit from therapy, which can help them to process the pain of loss and to develop new and stronger techniques for self-care and self-protection that they can implement in future relationships.

Most of the time, however, betrayed spouses want to salvage their damaged relationship. And if the addict is committed to living openly and honestly and behaving differently in the future, this is absolutely possible. If the cheated-on partner is also willing to engage in a process of healing and growing, this restoration is even more likely. Yes, it is often quite a while – typically a year or more – before relationship trust is fully reestablished, but couples who do survive one partner's sexual addiction often find that if they stick with the recovery process, their relationship can become more intimate and more meaningful than ever.

Dealing With Gaslighting

You don't have to feel stuck when you're dealing with gaslighting. Though sometimes it can feel like there's no way out, there are tips you can use in order to protect yourself from this abusive tactic. The following tips can help you find some solid methods for dealing with gaslighters effectively.

Believe In Your Intuition

Having a strong belief in what you think and what your senses perceive can stop gaslighters from pulling one over on you. If you know what you heard or saw and refuse to budge then they won't be able to control the situation to make it fit their desires.

It can be very hard to maintain that belief in yourself when they're making you feel crazy or try to convince you that you misread the situation. However, the more you can do it, the easier it will become and the less likely it will be that others will continue to try to gaslight you.

Recognize The Manipulation Patterns

Observing the patterns of gaslighting can help you to gain insight on when they happen, how they happen and why. While you're learning, you don't have to do anything about the gaslighting just yet, just observe and maybe try to think of ways that you can address it in the future.

While you're doing this, you can also consider recording the events that tend to be "erased" by the gaslighter after the fact. Writing it down, taking screenshots or recording the sound can give you proof of events that the gaslighter is trying to change for their own sake.

Preserve, Don't Win

Trying to win every battle with a gaslighter can become exhausting. Even if you catch them in their game at one instance, it doesn't necessarily mean that they will stop gaslighting. In some cases, it can be something that is embedded deep in their psyche, in combination with some kind of personality disorder or other issue.

Instead, focus on preserving yourself. Avoid wasting energy on them as much as possible. Instead of engaging a gaslighter, disengage and give your energy and attention to those who are healthy, respectful and caring. It will yield much greater rewards.

Understand That Changes Aren't Likely

In many cases, people who use gaslighting do so because it's one of the few ways they can get a sense of control over the world around them. Because of that, they aren't likely to stop at your request. This is one of the times when it's important to remember that you cannot change others.

If someone decides they want to stop engaging in the unhealthy behavior, then it's up to them to make those changes and stick with them. Consequently, it's also important to remember to set boundaries and to back away from a gaslighter if they are having negative effects on you.

Stay Strong

While it may not always help to fight back against someone who is gaslighting you, that doesn't mean you have to endure it or give them their way. Instead, find ways to disengage from them if you can.

If disengaging isn't an option, don't allow them to sway you. You know what you heard, saw or experienced and they don't have a right to try to change that. Refuse to give them their way, and don't let them erase the truth. If you do this, be prepared for them to lash out, as you're taking away their control.

Learn To Detach In A Healthy Way

When we become wrapped up in the gaslighting, it can start to eat away at our own concept of reality. As a result, it's a good idea to learn ways that you can detach from the experience. This may not mean detaching from life, or from the gaslighter as a whole but merely their attempt to change reality.

It can be helpful to trust in your perception of reality, and accept that it is true even if the gaslighter is trying their best to erase it. If they continue to press the matter, then disengage rather than allowing them to continue to mess with your mind. Otherwise, there can be negative consequences.

Be Realistic

It's important to see the situation, and the person using gaslighting, in a realistic way. Really consider the relationship and what you're getting from it. If aside from the gaslighting, the person is a positive presence in your life, then you may just need to learn how to deal with gaslighting when it happens.

However, if that person often leaves you doubting yourself or feeling badly, then don't try to rationalize the damage they are causing. Think about what is best for you in a solid, real way.

Remember That It Isn't Personal

For someone who is known for gaslighting others, the ability to erase and change the memories of others is comforting. It allows them to feel like they have some control over the situation, and can simply do away with any experiences that might have made them look badly.

Because of this, their gaslighting habit is less about trying to drive you crazy and more about controlling how they are viewed. It can help to remember that they do this because they are insecure and want to feel control, rather than just trying to make you look bad.

Consider Leaving The Relationship

Sometimes, when a person engages in emotionally and mentally abusive tactics like gaslighting, the best thing you can do is put distance between yourself in that person. No matter whether they're a coworker, friend, or even family member, your duty is to protect yourself.

This can depend on the person themselves and how they make you feel about yourself. If the gaslighting is just a small annoyance to you, and they tend to behave well otherwise then you may not need to take that step. However, if they often leave you confused or doubting yourself, it might be time to consider stepping away.

Gain Support

Finding support is one of the best ways that you can build up your strength and self confidence. As much as possible, surround yourself with people who are positive influences in your life. Oftentimes, these people can remind you that you aren't crazy, or the one who is in the wrong.

Consequently, they can help you to remain more grounded. If you're willing to take the step, the professional help of a therapist is also a great option to make use of. They can help you through your concerns and provide excellent tips on dealing with gaslighters.

Remember Your Self Worth

One of the easiest things to forget, but most important to remember, is that you don't deserve the gaslighting you receive. When someone behaves in an inappropriate or rude way and then tries to change the story later, don't let them twist the situation into becoming your fault, or you misreading something about it.

Furthermore, remember that you have no duty to put up with it. Your only duty is in taking care of yourself and your children if you have them. Don't let anyone convince you that you have to put up with the behaviors of gaslighters. You deserve to be treated in more respectful ways.

Learn, And Avoid

When you've learned the patterns of gaslighting in one individual, you can start to look for it in others you may come into contact with. Having this information on hand can really help you to avoid wasting energy on those who are going to try to erase or change events.

When you notice these behaviors in acquaintances, you can then re-route yourself to avoid spending too much time around them before it becomes more difficult to separate yourself. When you preemptively protect yourself, you can focus more on those who are positive influences in your life.

TRUSTING YOURSELF

How to Learn to Trust Yourself

The first and most important step in healing from gaslighting is learning to believe yourself. Building confidence in your own instincts and judgement is a skill we can all learn through daily practice. Here are some ways to start.

1. Practice mindfulness

Because gaslighting can alienate us from our own thoughts and feelings, the first step is simply listening. We can, learn to give ourselves time to feel the negative feelings that help us learn and heal.

Begin by noticing basic needs like hunger, tiredness, and thirst, rather than pushing them aside. Then, start taking a second to step back to notice your emotions. You don't have to change them or shame yourself for feeling them: simply validate your own experience.

2. Keep a feelings journal

Getting into the habit of recording what you're thinking and feeling every day can help you become more in-tune with your inner voice. You can notice patterns in your own thoughts and behaviors, and recognize what feelings dominate your life. It is okay to cry and be sad, but not if you do it all day. "Create timelines and monitor your emotions."

Journalling can also be a way of separating out your thoughts and feelings from the beliefs of the person who gaslit you. Journal and write a list of negative behaviors and patterns the gaslighter had. Then, we can write a list of positive things about ourselves and compare them.

3. Affirm your own feelings and opinions

If you're someone who seeks a lot of external validation from friends or partners, it can be useful to consciously practice validating and affirming yourself. It's okay to turn to supportive loved ones, but we can also learn to value ourselves from within.

Next time you have an urge to ask someone to validate a thought, perception, or feeling, take a moment to sit with it and affirm it for yourself instead. It may be difficult at first, but the more you practice, the more you will trust yourself.

4. Find professional support

Going to therapy, whether online or brick and mortar, is one of the best choices you can make to help yourself heal. The guidance of a therapist can accelerate the recovery process.

The right therapist can help you seperate your own thoughts, beliefs, and perceptions from those of the person who gaslit you, develop the tools to believe yourself, and support you as you heal from trauma.

You Can Heal Stronger

Healing can be challenging, and learning to trust yourself and others feels like taking a big leap into the unknown. But believing yourself is a muscle: the more you practice, the stronger you will get.

"Believe in yourself." "You are an amazing individual. We all have the power to heal and start living a happy life after a relationship where gaslighting was present." Your inner voice never abandoned you, it was just clouded out by someone else's opinions. And now that you are free of that influence, you can make your inner voice even stronger.

Printed in Great Britain
by Amazon